IMAGES
of America

WASHINGTON, D.C.
THE WORLD WAR II YEARS

Washington, D.C., was a city of occupation during World War II, albeit by its own forces. Armed military personnel protected significant structures, the National Mall, and the massive number of new city residents drawn to the area for patriotic duty. War production work in the many military facilities and newly formed civilian positions in the rapidly expanding federal government added to the influx of new residents in Washington. (NA.)

IMAGES
of America

WASHINGTON, D.C.
THE WORLD WAR II YEARS

Paul K. Williams

ARCADIA
PUBLISHING

Published by Arcadia Publishing
Charleston SC, Chicago IL, Portsmouth NH, San Francisco CA

Printed in the United States of America

Library of Congress Catalog Card Number: 2004100866

For all general information contact Arcadia Publishing at:
Telephone 843-853-2070
Fax 843-853-0044
E-mail sales@arcadiapublishing.com
For customer service and orders:
Toll-Free 1-888-313-2665

Visit us on the Internet at www.arcadiapublishing.com

President Franklin Roosevelt is seen here addressing a joint session of Congress and the nation on the day after the Pearl Harbor attack, December 8, 1941. He urged Congress to declare a state of war on the Japanese Empire, the first action that brought the city and the nation directly into ongoing wars in Europe and Asia. Marines with bayoneted rifles were stationed at every entrance of the Capitol building, and the D.C. Chief of Police placed 300 of his finest men among the fences, bushes, and trees on the Capitol grounds. (World Wide Photos, MLK Library.)

CONTENTS

ACKNOWLEDGMENTS

This book is dedicated to my parental units, Charles Norton and Nancy Kelsey Williams, who met just after World War II while my father worked at the Bureau of Standards in Cleveland Park and my mother worked in the baby department of a downtown department store before she was employed as a mathematician at the Naval Weapons Center, and was supervised by the recently immigrated German scientist Dr. Snay.

Acknowledgements must go to my partner Gregory J. Alexander, whose wit, love, and understanding of my time in the archives is priceless, as are his editing skills that have saved me from much embarrassment. Thanks goes to Barry Spencer, who put me in contact with war bride Nada Diana Coates for a fascinating view of the migration into the United States following the war. Thanks also goes to Peter L. Wolff, who has allowed me to publish "Scenes of the Past" in the *InTowner* newspaper for several years, and to his brother for providing a picture of their mother Lillian.

Most of the images in this volume were pulled by the staff at the Martin Luther King Jr. Memorial Library from their Washingtoniana Room. Pictures from other sources are noted in each caption, and include the Library of Congress, Prints and Photographs Department (LOC), The National Archives (NA), and individuals' and the author's private collection as noted. Every effort was made to identify the photographers' names and sources, and no image was intentionally left without an attribution.

The lights on the Capitol dome were turned off just two days after the attack on Pearl Harbor on December 7, 1941. The dome would remain dark until Germany surrendered in 1945, signifying to all that Washington, D.C., and its residents were constant targets during the raging war.

INTRODUCTION

This small tome cannot begin to explore all the intricacies and activities inherent in a large city facing the unthinkable: war and the threat of invasion or attack on its own soil. Many books, even volumes of books, have been written about the atrocities and military troop movements in Europe and the Pacific during World War II, and several outstanding books have been penned that focused exclusively on Washington, D.C., during the war years. Two that certainly deserve attention are Scott Hart's *Washington At War: 1941–1945*, published in 1970, and the widely read *Washington Goes to War* by journalist David Brinkley, published in 1988.

With the long anticipated and long overdue World War II Memorial opening on the National Mall on Memorial Day, 2004, however, the subject will again be on the tongues of the residents of the nation's capital and the entire country. This book cannot begin to detail the many fascinating, and sometimes secret, goings-on in Washington during the war, or the military activities themselves. Rather, it seeks to offer a broad overview of the period 1939–1945 told mostly through pictures, well over 200 in total, that have largely been a missing component in the books focusing on Washington, D.C., during this era. It is hoped that they might stimulate the reader to seek more information, or to satisfy a curiosity among younger generations to better understand their parents or grandparents.

On the morning of December 7, 1941, some Washingtonians were preparing to attend the Redskins-Eagles football game at the aging Griffith Stadium just outside LeDroit Park, while others were preparing to attend church or visit one of the many well-known museums. However, when the news about the attack on Pearl Harbor was broadcasted over the radio, many instead headed to the White House to offer their support to President Roosevelt.

Washington had begun preparing years earlier, however, to become involved in the European and Pacific conflicts. Temporary buildings were being constructed to house an ever-growing number of new residents and government workers, and new governmental agencies seemed to spring up overnight. The city's male population was waiting in long lines to register for the draft and to take their physical examinations, while many housewives prepared emotionally for their departure.

With the Japanese attack and the declaration of war, the city's residents went into true defense mode. Air-raid shelters were started, and Civilian Defense groups organized in nearly every neighborhood and outlying suburb. Washington's well-known townhouses were divided into rooming houses, while large estates turned over their once-lavish ballrooms for office use.

Washington residents had a rather rare first-hand view of the homefront aspect of World War II; they hosted government girls, were subject to rationing and restrictions, and planted urban Victory Gardens. They also could not have ignored the largest office building being built in their midst—the Pentagon. City residents could gather and listen to the President provide live updates on the war effort overseas, and could rally in their own backyards when either good or bad news about the fighting men and women was announced. They also lived with the fear that Washington, D.C., itself was a target and realistically a site of potential air raids by the enemy.

By highlighting the events of wartime Washington, D.C., through the use of historic images, this book is mostly arranged chronologically by subject matter. Major and minor events presented here are intended to amuse, record, and perhaps even surprise by focusing on a multitude of aspects, activities, and events that took place in Washington during World War II.

Military hardware used during World War II became a tourist curiosity both during and after the war. Mrs. Lillian Wolff from New York City is seen here proudly posing in front of a heavy artillery gun placed in front of the Smithsonian's Arts and Industries Building in April 1945, just one month before VE Day. (Photograph by Michael F. Wolff.)

One

PLANNING FOR WAR

Washington residents may have had their first hands-on experience in planning for war by the site of thousands of men lining up for the draft, most often held at the city's elementary and high schools beginning in 1940. Hundreds of temporary buildings were also being constructed on the National Mall, some of which had remained from World War I.

City residents, many of whom had experienced the ill effects of conservation in the previous war, also began hoarding items they feared might be rationed. Washington National Airport opened in June 1941, replacing the very dated Washington-Hoover Airport, which is now the site of the Pentagon. The new facility meant that members of Congress and the military could easily maneuver in and out of the city in the event of the looming crisis of war.

With news of the attack on Pearl Harbor on December 7, 1941, Washington's citizens mobilized for war. The Civilian Defense Corps were established, and air raid stations were built across the city, as mothers attempted to prepare emotionally for one or more of their sons to head overseas to fight.

There was also a concern for the country's priceless documents and works of art: the Declaration of Independence and the Constitution were moved from the Library of Congress to an underground vault in Fort Knox, and the priceless artworks at the National Gallery of Art were moved for safekeeping to the Vanderbilt estate in Asheville, North Carolina.

Americans who opposed getting involved in a looming conflict in Europe in the late 1930s were coined isolationists, seen here in front of the White House about 1940, and frequently protested the president. The most ardent supporter of "America First" was U.S. Senator Gerald P. Nye of North Dakota.

The flag at the German Embassy, then located on Massachusetts Avenue, N.W., just east of Thomas Circle, was lowered to half-staff on February 10, 1939, to mourn the death of Pope Pius XI. Viewed by many as an ally of Nazi Germany, the Pope had earlier signed a concord with Germany to secure the rights of Christians in the country because the Vatican recognized what a threat Hitler and his henchmen were to religious liberty.

Just prior to the war, the nation took notice of the tense, long-standing race relations when Howard University invited African-American singer Marian Anderson to perform in Washington in the spring of 1939, and intended her to sing at Central High School, then a white school in a segregated school system. The D.C. School Board rejected the venue, as did the Daughters of the American Revolution when Howard requested Constitution Hall. The Interior Department offered the steps of the Lincoln Memorial, where Anderson performed to a crowd of tens of thousands on Easter Sunday, 1939. The severely segregated city would partially and temporarily ease race restrictions in the coming years as thousands of government workers flocked to the city. (Acme Photo, LOC.)

Men are seen here lining up to register for the draft on October 16, 1940, at the Thomson School at Twelfth and L Street, N.W.

Many city residents reported to Fort Myer in Virginia for induction into the draft, as these men prepare for the physical evaluation. The institution of the draft caused the issuance of marriage licenses to nearly double in Washington, from 5,680 in 1939 to 10,554 in 1941, as men prepared to leave loved ones behind when they headed out of town for training and combat.

President Roosevelt stands at the speaker's podium at the first draft drawing held on October 29, 1940, at the War Department's auditorium. Seen holding the first draft capsule is Secretary of War Henry Stimson, while Lt. Col. Charles R. Morris unties his blindfold.

As early as April 1941, plans were being discussed to move both the Declaration of Independence and the United States Constitution from their display, which was then at the Library of Congress. During the evening of December 26, the documents, placed in a bronze container weighing about 150 pounds, were transferred under heavy guard to Union Station, and to a B&O Railroad Pullman car on the Eastlake. The next morning, the priceless artifacts reached their resting place for the duration of the war, a vault at Fort Knox in Kentucky. They were permanently installed at the National Archives on December 13, 1952, where each evening they are lowered 22 feet into a special vault, theoretically capable of withstanding even an atomic explosion. (NA.)

Washington National Airport went into operation in June 1941. It was a great engineering feat, as almost the entire facility was built atop land dredged from the Potomac River. The construction schedule for the terminal had been shortened in anticipation of the need for increased number of flights as tensions in Europe were escalating.

The main lobby of Washington National Airport's Administration Building was photographed shortly after it opened for business in June 1941. It then had just 170 employees, some of whom worked at the "progress board," tracking arriving and departing flights each day. Each of the 12 "loading stations" for planes and passengers featured a turntable that could turn the aircraft 180 degrees for departure from the terminal. (LOC.)

Reporters were treated to a behind-the-scenes view of the airport's automatic baggage handling system on opening day, June 22, 1941. The new airport replaced the Washington-Hoover Airport to the north, which was prone to flooding, often closing the airport for weeks at a time.

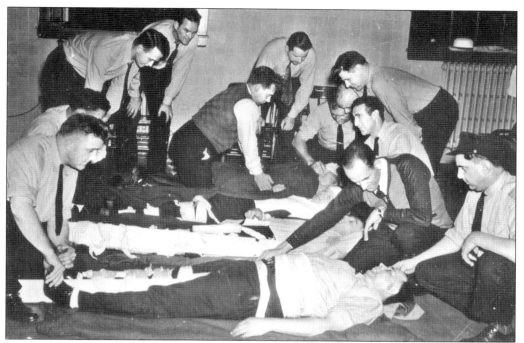

Many Washingtonians were preparing for an imminent involvement in the war, and the D.C. Fire Department began to offer first-aid training to its men in the spring of 1941 in preparation of an attack on the city itself.

Started as a typical garage construction project in the spring of 1941 at Linnaean Avenue and Porter Street, N.W., by owner Paul D. Crandall, the project was restyled to serve as an air raid shelter, with the owner anticipating a threat to the city in the coming years. This picture ran in the June 8, 1941, edition of the *Washington Star* newspaper.

Following the draft, Union Station became the scene of many men in uniform, awake and asleep, departing for duty stations and arriving for training and induction into a wide variety of defense jobs. Workers at the Traveler's Aid counter would sometimes tie a tag onto a sleeping soldier with the date and time of his departing train so that fellow passengers would ensure he was awakened in time to meet his train. These fellows appeared in the October 6, 1941, edition of the *Washington Star*.

The students at the Petworth School arranged their desks in a "V" for Victory when they were requested to do so by their teacher, Miss Nancy Kuykendall, two months before Germany and Italy declared war on the United States. The classroom was pictured in the *Washington Star* on October 15, 1941.

The city's first air raid shelter was opened at 4934 Indian Lane, N.W., on November 20, 1941. Seen here, from left to right, are Wilson B. Nairn, Col. S.F. Mashbir, Fred J. Eden, and Edward D. Hill. It was to be the first of dozens of such shelters located throughout the region.

This image portrays the interior of the Friendship (Tenleytown) Air Raid Shelter on November 20, 1941, which could have easily been mistaken for a military bunker deep in Europe. Pictured from left to right are Col. S.F. Mashbir, Deputy Warden Wilson B. Nairn, Fred J. Eden, and Edward D. Hill.

These gentlemen cover their ears in preparation for a test of the air raid siren atop a Washington building that would alert citizens to pending attack by enemy planes, and signaling blackout conditions. The sirens began to appear atop many of Washington's buildings.

On the morning of December 7, 1941, Japanese Special Envoy Saburo Kurusu, front, and Ambassador Admiral Kichisaburo Nomura requested a meeting with Secretary of State Cordell Hull at 2 p.m. Unbeknown to them, it was just about the same time the AP wire sent out a bulletin that Pearl Harbor had been attacked that morning at 7:35 a.m., Hawaiian time. Hull was said to have "cursed out" the two Japanese diplomats, seen here leaving the State Department after their meeting, headed to the Japanese Embassy. (UPI/Bettmann Photo, LOC.)

Just minutes after the AP wire announced the attack on Pearl Harbor, Japanese diplomats from all over Washington began arriving at their embassy at 2514 Massachusetts Avenue, N.W., in taxicabs, many without suit and tie. News reporters also gathered and recorded the occupants burning a large amount of paperwork in the interior courtyard before FBI agents arrived to protect the inhabitants. The building itself was designed by the architectural firm of Delano and Aldrich.

Washington residents gathered at the German Embassy on December 19, 1941, to witness its occupants preparing to leave the country; they left the embassy along Massachusetts Avenue, N.W., near Thomas Circle via the many motor coaches seen lining the street. Their building was placed under the ownership of neutral Switzerland for the duration of the war.

Downtown Washington is seen here moments before the test of a blackout drill on December 31, 1941. The same area seen below shows the impressive results of the drill, restricted to the interior of about 10 downtown blocks. Such blackouts had proven in Europe to make the landscape unfamiliar for enemy pilots seeking to drop bombs or incendiary devices.

With the attack on Pearl Harbor, efforts increased to prepare against such an occurrence in Washington. This December 23, 1941 image in Hecht's department store shows employees fitting black screens to be used when an air raid siren was heard indicating a blackout situation.

This image of President Roosevelt and Fiorello la Guardia was taken in 1943, two years after Eleanor Roosevelt had been sworn in as la Guardia's assistant in the Office of Civilian Defense. La Guardia had hesitantly accepted the post offered by Roosevelt and his aide Harry Hopkins to coordinate the agency, a somewhat awkward organization of dedicated, yet many times misguided civilians, young and old, who busied themselves looking skyward for enemy planes, preparing air raid shelters, and even teaching physical fitness. They took over the recently completed Dupont Circle Building for use as their headquarters. (LOC.)

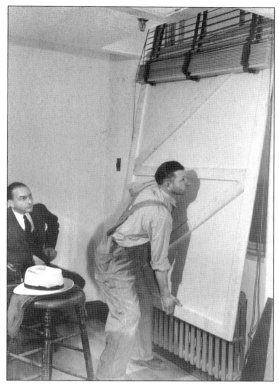

Two opposite offices, the Bundles for Britain and the America First organizations, were oddly located next to each other beginning in 1941, at 1710 and 1712 Connecticut Avenue, N.W., just north of Dupont Circle.

The Goodyear Blimp is seen here in the sky over the National Gallery of Art, just 15 days after it had been officially open by President Roosevelt on March 17, 1941. The gallery's masterpieces were quietly packed up in January 1942 out of concern for their safety and transferred by unmarked trucks to Biltmore, an estate outside of Asheville, North Carolina, that had been built by George Vanderbilt. Its remote locale in the mountains offered both security and a humidity-free climate for the artwork, which rested in a wing of the house under permanent guard until after the war.

Two

THE PENTAGON

The large open land just across the Potomac River in Arlington, Virginia, was chosen by Roosevelt to be the site of a temporary building complex needed to house the ever-growing numbers of wartime workers. A savvy colonel with political connections convinced Congress that a more permanent building was necessary, although built with a minimum of precious wartime materials, to consolidate the many branches of military offices that were renting space all over Washington at the beginning of 1941.

Efforts were stepped up to construct what would become the largest office building in the world—twice the square footage of the Empire State Building—soon after the attack on Pearl Harbor. With hundreds of architects, engineers, and draftsman working simultaneously with a construction crew that peaked at nearly 5,000, the Pentagon emerged in just 16 months. Its size was astounding—at its center was a five-acre courtyard where 40,000 workers could socialize and lunch. The building itself was a marvel, but despite its size—each side was over 950 feet long—conditions inside were still crowded. It was built with a series of ramps taking occupants to upper floors to minimize the need for precious metals required to produce elevators. It's not uncommon for workers, many who have worked there for years, to get lost in the building even today.

The building contains a staggering number of statistics, and even employs two people full-time just to change light bulbs. One of the must-do activities of new occupants is to find an elusive purple water fountain—the only one of the 685 fountains that is not white in color, seemingly hidden deep in an outer ring in the basement level, riddled with hallways that bend and shift endlessly.

The Pentagon also featured a self-contained shopping arcade, bookstore, medical facility, bank, and massive cafeterias, most of which remain to this day. The building was placed on the National Register of Historic Places as a National Historic Landmark, and was subject to an attack on September 11, 2001, exactly 60 years to the day that ground was broken for the facility.

Secretary of War Henry L. Stimson and Gen. George C. Marshall are seen here inspecting a European map in 1942. Faced with the new prospect of having to defend all of the western hemisphere, Stimson had earlier called for the construction of a single building to house all of the military departments, despite the massive temporary buildings already under construction in the city but quickly reaching capacity. He and General Marshall found and appointed the man who would become the father of the Pentagon, Brig. Gen. Brehon B. Somervell, who was appointed the Chief of Construction for the War Department in 1940. (LOC.)

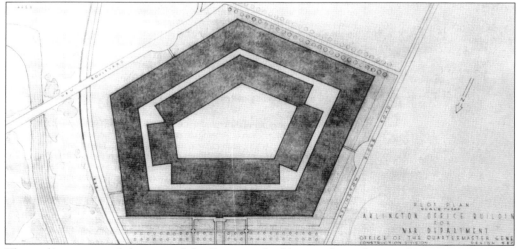

The earliest proposed drawing of the Pentagon building is this rather crude image, suggesting that its shape had evolved from the surrounding roads rather than a carefully calculated mathematical solution that was implemented to create an efficient building, despite its emergence as the world's largest office building. (LOC.)

General Somervell was a politically savvy individual and had anticipated a $6.5 million Congressional allocation for temporary buildings to be controversial in a July 17, 1941, committee hearing; he instructed his top engineers that same day to begin plans for a potential building to house an incredible 40,000 War Department workers, with their concepts due on July 21. The selected site was in Arlington, Virginia, just north of the newly completed Washington National Airport, which necessitated a building of five stories or less to minimize air traffic hazards. Thus Lt. Col. Hugh J. Casey, Col. Leslie R. Groves, and architect George Bergstrom produced the design concept and cost estimates for the largest building in the world in just three days. (LOC.)

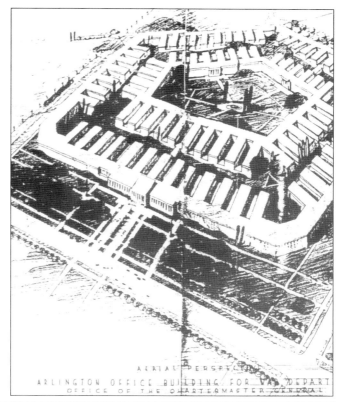

This aerial shot shows the land personally selected by President Roosevelt for the Pentagon, along the shores of the Potomac in Arlington where the old Washington-Hoover Airport was located (146.5 acres), as well as Arlington Farms (57 acres) and the Quartermaster Depot (80 acres). Another 160 individual parcels were added to bring the total construction site to 583 acres, just short of a square mile.

The chosen site of the Pentagon was partially occupied on the east by the old Washington-Hoover Airport, which was both prone to flooding and made obsolete by the construction of the new Washington National Airport to the south, which opened in June 1941. The flooding tendency of the land required massive land moving to fill 18 feet of soil and to level the site. (LOC.)

The Eastern Airlines hangar at the old Washington-Hoover Airport was converted into an office building for the exclusive use of the hundreds of designers, draftsmen, and engineers that were put to work creating the Pentagon. Arlington in 1940 was home to 57,000 residents, according to the census, and the construction of the Pentagon would add 40,000 new workers to the community, all housed in a single building that was to be twice the size of the Empire State Building. (NA.)

At the peak of construction activity, the Pentagon required the employment of 110 architects, 54 structural engineers, and 43 mechanical engineers, along with 444 draftsmen, all occupying a 23,000 square feet in the old Eastern Airlines terminal, seen here. Incredibly, the greatest part of the Pentagon's construction was completed by June 1942. It required the creation of 3,100 major architectural drawings, with construction often going on simultaneously with design, 24 hours a day.

While the Pentagon was still being designed in October 1941, the construction crew to prepare the site had grown to nearly 1,000 workers. Its original height of four stories had been raised to five, as additional government employees were anticipated. In all, 41,492 concrete piles were driven into the land even before the building's footprint had been established by the architects, each ranging from 27 to 45 feet in length; adding up to almost 200 total miles of pilings.

This massive wall-mounted model of the Pentagon and its surroundings was used for public relations efforts and shows its final design, with a riverfront esplanade extending over the George Washington Parkway. After all of the land had been assembled for the site, Virginia officially ceded it to the federal government in March 1942. The building carried a cost estimate of just over $31 million.

More than 25 major subcontractors were hired to work on the Pentagon. Full-scale work began on the building in August 1941, with its official ground breaking ceremony held on September 11 of that year; oddly, exactly 60 years later to the date, it was the site of the tragic terrorist attack of 2001. Interior floor space was estimated to be more than 6 million square feet, with a basement and mezzanine added to the design. By December 1941, 4,000 construction workers were employed in four shifts that operated 24 hours a day.

This cutaway view of the Pentagon reveals its ingenious design. By creating a pentagon shape with five concentric rings and intermittent light wells with connecting radial corridors, the design allowed for an individual to travel from one office to another in 17 minutes or less, despite its 17.5 miles of actual corridors! The design also dictated an office numbering system to allow for easy identification of locations in the building, with a combination of floor number (1-5), ring (A-E), and corridor number (1-10). Thus, an office numbered 5B269 was located on the fifth floor, B ring, between corridors 2 and 3.

The Pentagon was well under way when this construction image was taken in January 1942. Work schedules were stepped up due to the attack on Pearl Harbor a month previous, which had also necessitated a change in materials, as steel was critical for warships. Concrete was substituted, as were large wide ramps connecting floors instead of elevators and stairs. Incredibly for a building this size, only 13 elevators and 19 escalators were installed.

Wood forms were used to create the distinctive concrete patterns seen on the interior portions of the Pentagon today. Roosevelt had mandated that no marble be used; so the exterior was clad in limestone. An extraordinary number of bathrooms had been designed—280, comprising 4,900 individual toilets— not because of necessity but because Virginia law mandated separate facilities for white and black workers. The law was not enforced when the building opened for business.

Architect George Bergstrom was replaced by his assistant, David J. Witmer, in April 1942, when Bergstrom's position as President of the American Institute of Architects was terminated for "improper and unprofessional conduct." Witmer stayed on as architect during the many changes and challenges of the actual building construction. The Pentagon was originally envisioned only to be a post-war storage facility by Roosevelt, who had insisted that the floor load capacity be increased to accommodate the physical needs of millions of filing cabinets.

When it opened, the Pentagon featured the world's largest telephone switchboard, with 300 operators and supervisors employed to handle the tremendous number of calls. It was the equivalent of being able to handle a community of 125,000 persons. Another row of operators faced the row, pictured here on September 15, 1942, with an additional row of operators seated at a long row of tables in the middle.

The enormity of the Pentagon can really only be comprehended when one looks at one side at a time, whose length at 960 feet could accommodate the length of three U.S. Capitol buildings. In all, the building featured 7,748 windows of varying size, 685 drinking fountains, and 4,200 clocks when it opened in 1942.

Entire rooms at the Pentagon were designated as filing rooms, such as this one seen here. More sensitive departments were housed in the basement levels, where the lack of windows ensured that their work remained top secret. The building features its own printing plant and shredding facility so that most top-secret documents never leave the facility.

The Pentagon featured a bus lane directly in the building when it opened, shuttling workers to and from work, as well as to other defense-related facilities in and around Washington. In 1942, approximately 10,000 workers arrived at the building by Capital Transit buses from Washington, with an additional 4,000 arriving from Virginia; 8,000 preferred to drive and park their own private automobiles in the 54 acres of parking surface.

The final authorization of $35 million did not provide any funds for the exterior landscaping or vast parking lots surrounding the Pentagon, nor the riverfront esplanade, ceremony grounds, and separate heating plant, which itself covered more than an acre. The intricate roadways and access ramps resulted in 30 miles of new highways, 3 cloverleaf exchanges, and 15 overpasses. The total expenditure was finalized at $85 million.

In May 1942, just six months after groundbreaking, War Department workers were able to move into two of the five sections of the Pentagon and found ample food and beverages available in one of the large self-ordering cafeterias, seen here. Occupation rose to 7,000 by June, 10,000 by July, and 22,000 by December 1942.

The Pentagon featured a main concourse that had virtually every business and service that most small communities boasted in their downtowns, including a branch of the famed Woodward & Lothrop store, pictured here. Other services included a bookstore, bank, dry-cleaning, barber, pharmacy, and medical clinic.

On Christmas Day 1942, 15,000 workers gathered in the central courtyard of the Pentagon to sing Christmas carols, being especially careful not to venture off the sidewalks and pathways. Incredibly, the building housed 22,000 workers after just 16 months of construction. Many worked on Christmas Day due to the travel restrictions imposed on residents.

Thousands of Pentagon employees descended into the five-acre center courtyard each lunch hour to enjoy a bit of fresh air and a park-like setting. The tented area in the center was later replaced with a permanent lunch counter coined "Ground Zero Café" by its employees. Hundreds of Adirondack chairs ringing the center are still used by employees today to take a brief refreshing nap.

The vast parking lots surrounding the Pentagon are partially built over levels of the building that are completely underground. By June 1942, nearly 7,000 War Department employees had been transferred to the building, most of who arrived in their own automobiles.

Secretaries at work in the Pentagon are seen here in 1943. A year later, toward the end of the construction period, it was decided to add additional space on the fifth floor, adding 350,000 square feet of office space under the roof portion of the inner rings. That decision delayed the official opening to January 15, 1943, although it had been occupied as early as May 1942.

Pentagon employees are seen here on the riverfront esplanade during a fire drill in 1943. The area was commonly reserved for a variety of ceremonial duties and lectures. It also led to the Potomac River and a small marina for military personnel. Today, employees make more than 200,000 phone calls from the building, drink over 30,000 cups of coffee, and consume 6,800 soft drinks from vending machines located in the facility.

Over the years, the Pentagon has updated its various individual service war rooms as technology improved, as well as created a joint "War Room" at the center of the building in which all service activities are tracked and threats to the United States are interpreted.

The massive exodus every day from the Pentagon, seen here about 1945, led to the formation of "slug lines" still used today, where a line forms with uniformed and civilian personnel on the ramp headed south into Virginia, for example; drivers with spare room pick up employees and drive them to their homes in exchange for a few dollars. (LOC.)

Despite its reputation for an elite place of work today, overcrowding has been a problem in the Pentagon since its initial opening. The lack of privacy amongst workers is still of concern to this day, even following a five-year period of renovation in the late 1990s. Contractors and non-military personnel are not routinely counted in its overall population, sometimes estimated at close to 45,000 individuals.

With the war over, and a new civilian military position created known as the Secretary of Defense, the first individual with that title, James Forrestal, moved into the Pentagon. He and subsequent Secretaries of Defense have occupied this lavish office suite on the E ring since September 22, 1947. (NA.)

With the formation of the Air Force as a separate entity of the Department of Defense in 1947, it also formed its own war room in the Pentagon. Seen here is the room where the top Air Force officers would gather, with an illuminated map of North America at the end of the room. Behind the drapes were additional detailed maps of the world's hot spots. The soundproof room was entered via a heavy steel safe door with combination lock, like that typically found in the city's banking institutions.

Portions of the Pentagon that require an additional level of security and identification to enter have always been restricted, even to regular employees. Here, a guard is seen watching over such an area in 1951.

Three

DEFENDING WASHINGTON

The attack on the United States at Pearl Harbor in 1941 quickly changed the way Washingtonians viewed their city, now suspect to possible attack itself. The military was quick to mount a variety of antiaircraft guns in and around the city, protecting both its residents and its well-known monuments and institutions. Hundreds of Army troops from nearby Fort Myer soon occupied the city, beginning with Roosevelt's speech at the Capitol declaring war.

Congress ordered an emergency measure to turn off the spotlights shining on the city's most recognizable structures, including the White House, the Capitol, and the Washington Monument, for the duration of the war. Air-raid wardens were established, and civilian air raid centers were set up in most of the city's many neighborhoods. Blackout curtains were also installed on most government buildings and in private homes, and the Sunday drone of the air raid testing signal soon became a constant reminder of a country at war. Stage Door Canteens were held at the Belasco Theater to raise money and morale, while children of all ages were taught how to conserve and to protect themselves in bunkers built at many of the local schools.

People of German and Asian decent were eyed suspiciously, and residents often occupied themselves keeping a watchful eye out for saboteurs and foreign spies. Foreign embassies lining Sixteenth Street and Massachusetts Avenue that represented countries under Germany's control fell silent, their well being placed under the control of the neutral Swiss government.

Washington also became a city of wartime manufacturing, with the Navy Yard producing hundreds of 16-inch gun barrels, and its ports and military bases actively shipping out men in uniform or unloading the caskets of those that died fighting overseas. The overall feeling of the city during the war was that of a patriotic duty to do everything one could in order to both support our troops and to keep the city's residents safe from attack.

Few people knew that during the war years, President Roosevelt had a bunker made available to him in Vault Number One in the adjacent Treasury Building. The bunker was created by the U.S. Secret Service following the attack on Pearl Harbor, along with the erection of the heavy iron fence around the White House lawn. Access to the bunker was via a 741-foot-long underground passageway from the White House to the Treasury Building; it was equipped with 12 telephone lines, food, and ample room for Roosevelt and top members of his staff. The only time it was used was when Winston Churchill traversed its length to avoid reporters on his visit to Washington. (NA.)

Following the Japanese attack on Pearl Harbor, the federal government went about protecting Washington's well-known landmarks as well as its residents. A total of 38 marines were allotted to the Washington Aqueduct and sent to guard the Main Navy and Munitions Building, a temporary structure on Constitution Avenue, N.W., that dated from World War I. Military personnel are seen here lurking in the shadow of the Lincoln Memorial on December 8, 1941, with their guns protecting the Arlington Memorial Bridge.

Army personnel are seen here pointing their mobile antiaircraft gun above the Arlington Memorial Bridge when this image was taken on December 8, 1941. Later, larger guns were placed at either end of the bridge, but they were fabricated of wood, meant to fool the enemy into thinking the bridge was heavily protected.

An unidentified gentleman, in December 1941, demonstrates a kit that each American was encouraged to create that would assist in the event of an air raid. Meanwhile, marine guards were stationed at all Washington utility facilities to avert any threat of sabotage.

Air-raid wardens in Kalorama demonstrate the neighborhood's ability as the only area to date that was capable of providing gas masks for all its inhabitants when this picture appeared in the January 6, 1942 issue of the *Washington Star* newspaper.

Miss Lowella Temple and Miss Eleanor Winget stop to view one of the cut-off switches installed on streetlights in case of air attacks. This one was installed in January 1942 at the intersection of Eighteenth and G Streets, N.W.

The February 1942 "Victory Book" campaign at Western High School collected about 7,000 books that were sent to troops overseas for recreation and leisure. Seen here are, from left to right, Leonard Abel, Mary Lane, Richard Blough, Margaret Monteith, Jerome Stenger Jr., Antoine Miller, and Martha Reed.

These Bolling Field privates, who couldn't wait until the end of the Victory Book Campaign on February 4, 1942, collected a part of their share in January of that year from the public library at Eighth and K Streets, N.W. Lifting books are Pvt. Robert Taylor, at left, and Pvt. Francis Gehant, at right, and in the truck Pvt. William Brown, at left, and Pvt. Bernard Sumner, at right, all of the Army Signal Corps.

The Victory Book Campaign in Washington in early 1942 netted over 7,000 books that were distributed to Navy and Marine bases worldwide. Seen at left is Isabel DuBois, Navy Librarian, and Mrs. Philip S. Smith, District Victory Book Campaign Director, overlooking the pickup at the southwest branch of the D.C. Public Library. Loading books are, from left to right, Eugene Cornwell, Seaman Raymond Russell, Pvt. Walter Wosotowsky, and Cpl. Perry Fischer.

Strategic wartime materials had been eliminated from the manufacture of this "Victory" bicycle, which was demonstrated in Washington in March 1942. Leon Henderson, administrator of the Office of Price Administration, is seen here providing a ride to work with his secretary, Miss Betty Barrett. (LOC.)

The building at 1341 Maryland Avenue, N.E., served as the city's headquarters for the air raid wardens. Seen here are, from left to right, Lt. Col. H.O. Atwood, Mary Mason, Assistant Chief Air Raid Warden J.C. Varah, Switchboard Operator Elsie Ramby, and G.R. Lyles.

With most of the younger residents, and even police themselves, drafted into action, older city residents were trained and acted as an auxiliary police force and stationed throughout the city in volunteer shifts.

Mrs. Kathryn Brivker, principal of Somerset Elementary School, explains to her students the purpose of air raid protection barricades, built of large logs and placed on the lower level of the city schools by volunteers. Seen here are, from left to right, Donald Pugh, age 7; Jimmy Riggleman, 9; George Pugh, 9; Brivker; Scott Bowers, 8; and Bryant Kingsbury, 9. Their picture appeared in the *Washington Star* on March 2, 1942.

Senate District Committee chairman McCarran, left, with James M. Landis, center, and Office of Civil Defense and city commissioner John Russell Young, right, were photographed riding around the city streets on March 4, 1942, testing the blackout effort of city residents and business owners. The day following the Pearl Harbor attack, Young had encouraged Washingtonians to "complete the Air-Raid Warden Service by delivering . . . the names of men and women [needed] to complete all air raid warden sectors of the city; select a well-qualified woman to organize emergency feeding units; and to select a well qualified man or woman to organize emergency housing services."

This mobile air raid siren was lifted onto the top of a building just south of Franklin Square, N.W., on April 21, 1942, as part of the city's air raid system.

Students of all ages participated in the Civilian Defense effort; these youngsters did their part handing out informational leaflets in the Kalorama neighborhood.

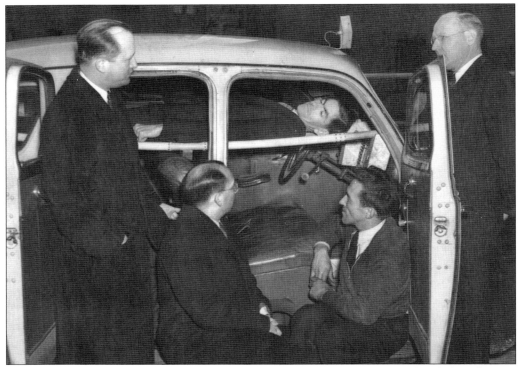

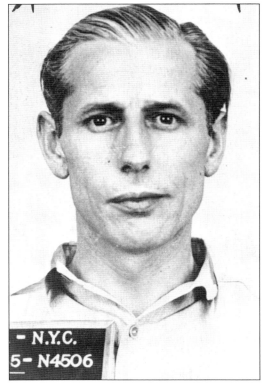

Area cab companies retrofitted their fleet with these stretchers to be used in the event of an air raid or other emergency as auxiliary ambulances.

Washingtonians discovered just how vulnerable the nation was to attack with the news that George John Dasch, part of two German teams that had come onto American soil from German U-Boats to sabotage various targets, had been arrested at the Mayflower Hotel on June 27, 1942. Details were not released until years later, but Dasch and four others had come ashore on Long Island on June 12 and narrowly escaped detection, while another group landed in Florida four days later. It is unclear why Dasch decided to betray his country, but he broke with his group and made his way to Washington, where he called the FBI to his hotel room, apparently thinking he would be heralded as a hero. Following a military trial for all eight individuals at the Supreme Court, they were electrocuted on August 8, 1942. Seen here is the official FBI mug shot of Dasch, taken on June 29, 1942. (LOC.)

Mr. and Mrs. Harvey Brown of Mount Rainier, Maryland, trained area firehouse mascots as part of the "Dogs for Defense" program. Driver R. Basford is seen here in July 1942 delivering "Buddy" to the Browns, who would then train him for two months before he was shipped off to the Army. After the war, dogs returned to their original firehouses.

Actress Marlene Dietrich is seen here moments before a patriotic radio broadcast from the Main Navy and Munitions Building along Constitution Avenue, N.W., in 1942. At her left is an Army officer assigned to censor her script if necessary, and at right is a civilian carefully timing her performance. Other multi-starred USO performances were held on the steps of the Treasury Building. (LOC.)

On August 13, 1942, 22 people graduated from Defense Class as emergency feeding and housing wardens, including a 65-year-old grandmother and a 13-year-old boy. Seen here are, from left to right, Mrs. Nellie Holmes, the Assistant Director of Civil Protection Training Schools; Mrs. Lillian David, age 65; Mrs. Ruth Fox; Capt. William L. Clemens; and Douglas Greenwalt, age 13.

The *Washington Star*, like many businesses in Washington, turned the information booth in the lobby of its building over to the Navy, which used it as a recruiting center throughout the war. It was pictured here in the *Star* on August 30, 1942. Earlier that summer, word had spread that actor Clark Gable had taken his physical examination at Bolling Field in Southeast Washington.

Weekly NEWS REVIEW

Volume XX, Number 35   WASHINGTON, D. C.   May 22, 1942

Africa's Role in Struggle Is Growing in Importance

United Nations Now in Control of Most Vital Regions of Continent. Fate of Vichy-France's Possessions Creates Most Serious Problems

GERMAN and Russian armies are locked in deadly combat on several fronts (see page 3). The big question now is: "Can the Germans be stopped, or will they sweep through to the rich oil fields in the region of the Caucasus Mountains, and then on to the Near East?"

This question will be answered during the summer months. The battles which are beginning to take place will show whether Germany still has the power to win great victories after her long winter of reverses on the Russian front.

In the campaigns which lie ahead, the vast continent of Africa—5,000 miles long and 4,500 miles across at its widest point—is certain to play a very large part—perhaps a decisive one. Already, it is serving the cause of the United Nations in a number of important ways. Germany, Italy, and Japan realize this, but thus far they have not been able to do much about it. The bulk of

Man of the Week
Aviation Leader

The *Weekly News Review* newspaper was published at 744 Jackson Place in Washington and was aimed at educating students across America. It was published weekly during the school year, and classrooms could order a full subscription for $1.20 per year in 1942. Its editor that year was Walter E. Myer. (Author's private collection.)

The Washington Stage Door Canteen opened up at the Belasco Theater on the east side of Lafayette Square in September 1942 for entertaining the area's troops. Seen here at a fund-raising dinner on August 7 of that year are actress Tallulah Bankhead, Milton Shubert, and First Lady Eleanor Roosevelt at the National Theater. Mrs. Anna Roosevelt Boettiger, daughter of the President, won the raffle ticket for a $185 Hattie Carnegie dress.

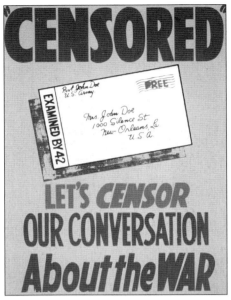

Within two weeks of the attack on Pearl Harbor, President Roosevelt selected Byron Price, executive editor of the Associated Press, to head a new Office of Censorship. The office would censor mail and cables entering and leaving the country, and would urge the press, voluntarily, to withhold information useful to the enemy. The office employed nearly 14,000 censors almost immediately upon its creation. (LOC.)

The staff of the French Embassy was photographed leaving their embassy in Sheridan Kalorama on November 17, 1942, for the second time. Earlier, in 1940, when France was occupied by the Germans, they sent a puppet of the Nazi regime named Gaston Henry-Haye to Washington to act as ambassador. His mission was to attempt to keep America out of the war and to spread propaganda masking the intent of the German government. Instead, his telephones were tapped, his whereabouts monitored, and his agents watched continuously to ensure ineffectiveness. The Vichy government in France broke relations with Washington in November 1941, and Secretary of State Cordell Hull had him deported. (UPI/Bettmann Photo, LOC.)

Union Station, seen here in November 1942, was the principal point of departure for World War II officers headed to the city and for servicemen who were heading out for basic training. The station's USO lounge offered servicemen cookies, cakes, refreshments, and other sundries free of charge.

Members of the Junior Commando Unit were recognized by Frederick Stanton, administrative assistant to the President of Howard University. The institution sponsored 11 African-American boys that lived in the vicinity of the school to instill patriotism in the young followers. Seen here on December 13, 1942, are, from left to right, J. Linn Hope, age 4, mascot of the unit; "General" Kaye Dunham, age 9; "Major General'" Edward S. Hope, age 7; and G. Frederick Stanton of Howard University.

This test of Washington's blackout drill was taken from the rooftop of the Printcraft building about 1943 by a photographer working for the Office for Emergency Management. The sirens were operated on Sundays every three months to test the preparedness of Washingtonians to comply with blackouts. (LOC.)

These sailors were photographed enjoying the Japanese cherry trees on the tidal basin about 1943. Four of the famous trees had been vandalized following the Japanese attack on Pearl Harbor, prompting the National Park Service to take additional precautions in security. The Jefferson Memorial, seen in the background, was the only memorial completed during the war, and was dedicated by President Roosevelt on April 13, 1943, with a plaster statue of Jefferson by sculptor Rudolph Evans inside the rotunda that stood in place until a bronze replacement could be installed following wartime restrictions on metal. (NA.)

Washington, D.C., firefighters display their ladder trucks in front of the United States Capitol in a "V" for Victory when this image was taken for the *Washington Daily News* in May 1943.

Prime Minister Winston Churchill and President Roosevelt were photographed with their military chiefs of staff at the White House during Churchill's second visit to the nation's capital in June 1942. He and Roosevelt conferred on the course of action required by the United States to fight two fronts concurrently in Europe and the Pacific. (UPI/ Bettmann Photo, LOC.)

Many African Americans in Washington were justly angered by the fact that their young men were being drafted, yet faced discrimination at home, with the news that the local Capitol Transit Company maintained a policy of not hiring black motormen. This integrated and organized protest took place on the city streets in May 1943.

The stand opposite the District Building on Pennsylvania Avenue was staffed in the summer by Washington Debutants, who handed out stamps and stickers informing residents how they could conserve gasoline.

These couples watched and listened to summer concerts held at the shore of the Lincoln Memorial from their canoes. The venue was the popular Water Gate floating stage anchored off the west side of the Lincoln Memorial. The 65-member National Symphony Orchestra performed under the direction of Dr. Hans Kindler for most of the war years. (LOC.)

With their janitor drafted, these students from Montgomery Blair High School in Maryland volunteered to clean their classrooms at the end of each school day. They formed a Voluntary School Victory Corps as part of their War Mobilization Program. Pictured are, from left to right, Gloria Cann, Eddie Stock, and Joan Foley.

These salesgirls at the Woodward & Lothrop store do their part, selling savings stamps to city residents. Between July 1, 1941, and June 30, 1946, the Bureau of Engraving and Printing produced more than 8 billion savings stamps of various denominations with a total face value of $1.7 billion.

These Chinatown children were photographed selling War Bonds on their front steps. Many Chinese residents were fearful of being mistaken as Japanese and subjected to harassment and public disdain. The United States Treasury enlisted the help of newspaper boys to sell War Bonds during their rounds, which turned out to be a huge success. Contests were also held between papers to compete for the honor of selling the largest number of bonds.

These Royal Air Force Cadets, training in the United States, broadcasted messages to their families in the United Kingdom from the Washington affiliate of the NBC Studios, which was then located in the art deco-styled Trans-Lux Theater at Fourteenth Street and New York Avenue, N.W.

The Traveler's Aid booth at Union Station assisted hundreds of thousands of soldiers that came in and out of the station during the war years, who quite possibly made up questions when it was staffed with such young and beautiful women as the one seen in this image.

The National Aeronautics Association, through its model division, the Academy of Model Aeronautics, founded an Air Youth Division during the war to encourage youth to become involved in various aspects of flight. These youngsters are seen here at the Modelhaven Airport, between Baltimore and Washington, about 1944. It was noted that the builders of models in the past were then putting their skills to work in America's war production factories. (LOC.)

Taken in June 1944, this image shows military personnel on the roof of the Government Printing Office with 40mm antiaircraft guns protecting the city from an air raid. It was one of dozens of locations atop the city's tallest buildings, and it was a common site to see armed military personnel riding in the elevator along with office workers, headed to their posts at rooftop stations.

The sign posted likely did not have to remind the man on watch at this 40mm gun on the roof of the Interior Building in June 1944, protecting the Washington Monument and other Mall landmarks. Walton Onslow, an Interior Department employee, recalled one occasion where he heard the gun firing rounds, fearing the city was under attack. Unbeknownst to him, a security officer at the Lincoln Memorial reported an attack on the Mall; it turned out, however, that the gun had gone off accidentally, hitting the top portion of the Lincoln Memorial.

These military personnel are seen on the roof of the Government Printing Office in June 1944 with a 40mm antiaircraft gun and a .50-caliber water-cooled AA machine gun protecting the skies over the city.

Seen on the East Potomac Golf Course in June 1944 manning a 40mm antiaircraft gun are, from left to right, Pvt. Theodore Laurence, Pvt. Adam Bednarz, Cpl. Lewis Wilds, Roscoe Pool, and Sgt. Elmer Stiffler.

On November 19, 1944, Washingtonians welcomed President Roosevelt back to the city, seen here with Vice President Elect Harry Truman (center) and Vice President Henry Wallace (right), following their election victory, Roosevelt's fourth term in office. He joked with reports that day when he stated, "I hope that some of the scribes in the papers won't intimate that I expect to make Washington my permanent residence."

Four

RATIONING, SCRAP DRIVES, AND VICTORY GARDENS

Shortly after the city's residents recovered from the news of the attack on Pearl Harbor, they were subject to the first rationings of gasoline and rubber, both imports having been curtailed by the German submarine activity. The Office of Price Administration (OPA), headed by Leon Anderson, would eventually include 20 items it controlled for rationing, including sugar, flour, meat, chickens, metal, and the most coveted vice, the cigarette. It was said that smokers would not dare to reveal their full pack in public, fearful that somebody might ask to bum a cigarette, and instead would discreetly pull them from a coat jacket one at a time.

The OPA grew to an agency of 60,000 workers, overseeing the rationing program, as well as curbing speculation, and cracking down on black market activity. When it was announced that gas was to be rationed, Washingtonians lined up by the thousands to horde gasoline, with most of the city's stations running dry. By May 1942, it was clear that voluntary rationing was not being effective, and mandatory rationing was institutionalized. Rationing cards became commonplace, as did long lines at the supermarket and the gas station, where most had to do with only two gallons of fuel per week. Clothing dyes were curtailed, needed for military uniforms, which meant that Washington's women entered a period of years where wearing drab colors meant a patriotic duty.

While speed limits were lowered to "Victory Speed"—35 miles per hour—Washingtonians also began collecting metal and scrap rubber for the war effort. All over town, huge piles of scrap were seen, with a metal pail or bucket all that was necessary for entrance into the famed Griffith Stadium. Youngsters joined in the collecting for fun and profit, while the huge influx of government workers, many from farming communities, began to plant Victory Gardens on almost every available plot of land, no matter how small. The mentality at home was conservation and saving for those loved ones fighting in Europe and the far-off Pacific theater.

Washingtonians got used to long lines throughout the war years; this one for the issuance of 1941 license plates took place at Pennsylvania Avenue and Sixth Street, N.W.

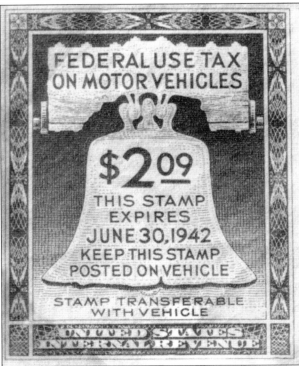

FEDERAL USE TAX ON MOTOR VEHICLES

$2.09

THIS STAMP EXPIRES JUNE 30, 1942 KEEP THIS STAMP POSTED ON VEHICLE

STAMP TRANSFERABLE WITH VEHICLE

UNITED STATES INTERNAL REVENUE

Automobiles used during the war years were subject to a federal use tax and required that this stamp be affixed to the windshield. This particular stamp was issued on January 15, 1942.

In May 1942, it was apparent that volunteer rationing was not effective, and Washington's public schools were closed for three days to be made available as distribution points for mandatory rationing cards. Teachers were instructed to serve as clerks during the period, handing out cards to the city's 125,000 drivers based on a tier system of drivers' needs and occupations. Seen here is the immense line formed around Coolidge High School for gasoline ration cards, taken on May 13, 1942. (NA.)

Gasoline rationing and creativity resulted in the "sedanbus" seen here in front of the Capitol. It was the result of cutting in half an ordinary 1942 five passenger four door sedan, and inserting a plastic and wood center section that could accommodate an additional five seats. It was manufactured by the Fitzjohn Coach Company of Muskegon, Michigan, and cost about $1,000.

These Washingtonians were photographed in December 1942 lining up for as many as 20 different ration cards for items all issued by the War Price and Rationing Board Rations Line. Gasoline and rubber were among the first items rationed, then eventually other items in short supply such as sugar, flour, and meat, all of which resulted rather unexpectedly in the publication of myriad cookbooks that included recipes for meals that could be cooked using only non-rationed items. (NA.)

The government even instituted a program to teach school children the value and intricacies of rationing, with the belief that the education would be brought home to their parents. Here, youngsters at Parkview Elementary School in Northwest Washington are seen in their school demonstration of the Office of War Information project in February 1943.

Harvey's Restaurant was located at 1107 Connecticut Avenue, N.W., beginning in 1932, and along with the Occidental Grill, it was one of only two restaurants excluded from meat rations by President Roosevelt during the war years; mainly so that it could serve a good meal to various high ranking military officials. The restaurant was established in 1858 by George and Thomas Harvey, who pioneered a safe method of consuming oysters. Cartoonist Thomas Nast illustrated George Harvey, seen here, about 1880. Bean soup was then a tradition in the city and a must-have with nearly every visitor, who often wrote home that they had at long last "eaten Capitol bean soup."

Government workers in Washington utilized the War Wagon Trailer sponsored by the Office of Defense Transportation. Constructed of wood and masonite on a steel frame, it offered a ride to 24 passengers and conserved materials and fuel in a body only 12 feet long. Conversely, an average city bus, which measured 32 feet long, held 40 passengers. This war wagon was photographed on February 12, 1943.

Even clothing and fashion were subject to wartime rationing, as these gentlemen show off the popular zoot suit at Uline Arena during a Woody Herman Orchestra performance. Restrictions on cloth halted the two-year reign of the popular new suit style, which was considered to waste an abundance of cloth. Dyes for clothing were also restricted, used for the production of uniforms, which resulted in slow fading of bright colors from men's and women's fashions. (LOC.)

V-Mail was a method invented to send regular mail correspondence to and from armed forces around the world by transferring them to a type of microfilm; 1,600 letters could be placed on a roll of film a little larger than a pack of cigarettes. Special readers allowed personnel to read their letters at overseas bases. (LOC.)

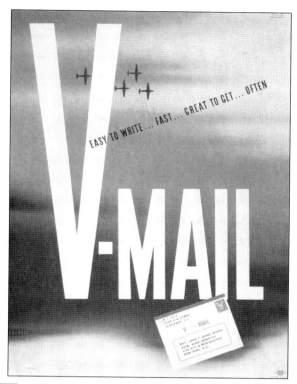

This patriotic poster urged Americans to send their binoculars to the U.S. Naval Observatory to be recycled into wartime materials. It was located on Massachusetts Avenue, N.W., on the site of what is today the official residence of the Vice President. (LOC.)

LICK THE PLATTER CLEAN

Don't Waste FOOD

The "Share a Ride" program was an outstanding success in saving gas and materials for the war effort. Seen here at the AAA headquarters is Miss Laura Flogel, registering for a ride, and Gorman Springer, registering his car for riders. John M. Waters Jr., an AAA representative, looks on.

The Government Printing Office produced this poster in 1944 of nursery rhyme characters Jack Sprat and his wife with a clean platter, encouraging citizens not to waste any food scraps during the war effort. It was issued by the War Food Administration. One of the most acute shortages was that of sugar, as the United States then imported nearly 70 percent of its stock, and the government feared that the ships carrying it would soon be converted into military use, cutting off the supply. (LOC.)

Not every citizen and business owner happily conceded to a curfew enacted by the area War Manpower Commission (WMC) that called for all establishments to close at midnight. The owners of the Lamplighters Club opened after midnight, and claimed they were therefore exempt from the curfew; seen here at 2 a.m. on March 7, 1945, are revelers who sought to gain admittance by means of the membership cards.

Paul E. Bauer shows what city residents needed to get along during the war years in Washington, including a draft registration and classification; A and B gas rations and punch card; war rations books 1, 2, and 3; fuel oil rations; token points; tire inspection card; and civil defense and Red Cross identification cards.

Incidentally, long lines continued long after the end of the war had been declared, as hundreds of persons lined up at the Super Freeze Market at 723 Eleventh Street, N.W., on January 17, 1946, to buy scarce frozen hams, bacon, and other meats. This was despite the fact that most items became point free in 1944, with the exception of butter, sugar, and canned fruit.

Patriotic slogans and campaigns that would be considered slanderous today encouraged Washingtonians to donate materials for the war effort, as did this one with the slogan "Slap the Japs with Your Rubber Scraps." Manpower and rationing mandated many area hotels to limit guests to one towel a day and a change in bed linen only once per week.

Impromptu piles of scrap iron began appearing all over the city's streets, piled high with a variety of household items.

Capt. Richard H. Mansfield assists Janet Rogers, who lived at 529 1/2 Ninth Street, N.E., with her contribution to the scrap metal drive. Their image appeared in the local paper on July 24, 1941.

These boy scouts were photographed on Halloween 1941, playing in the results of their aluminum scrap drive in Washington.

Used metal license plates were one of the many items saved for scrap.

Scrap collection piles were often found at local gas stations. This one, photographed on July 1, 1942, featured cartoons of German and Japanese leaders, with slogans aimed at encouraging donations. Even the National Zoo joined in the effort, donating a 700-pound outmoded bear cage in 1942.

Spectators at Griffith Stadium at Seventh and U Street, N.W., were admitted to a variety of sporting events if they contributed to the scrap pile at the entrance gates. This image appeared in the *Washington Star* on August 25, 1942.

If you could not carry your scrap metal to one of the many piles throughout the city, you could wait for a patriotic soul to come by with his truck to gather up your contribution. Scrap drives saw a marked increase of donations when it was announced that the United States had begun a bombing campaign on Tokyo, Japan in April 1942.

Known as the largest wrought and cast iron gates on any private residence in Washington, these adorning the driveway of Friendship, the summer home of Edward and Evalyn Walsh McLean on Wisconsin Avenue, N.W., were sold for scrap in 1942. Government officials can be seen inspecting the treasure on the site of what is today McLean Gardens apartments.

Metal objects from the Friendship estate were gathered by the Defense Homes Corporation, which acquired the estate and grounds from the McLean family. Several statues, including those seen at the right, were to be evaluated before being scrapped, seen here awaiting inspection on September 20, 1942.

Children of all ages gathered scrap as a patriotic pastime, scouring alleys and streets where residents had put out scrap goods for collecting.

Many of Washington's cast iron fences, balconies, and other architectural features were replaced with wooden counterparts throughout the war years, in an effort to show patriotism by donating such materials to scrap drives. Airplane production, meanwhile, reached a record level of 9,000 units by November 1943, averaging one new warplane every 4 minutes and 48 seconds that month.

A Victory Garden was planted by gas station-owner Harry W. Coleman and his attendant Harry J. Blake, seen here watering the tiny garden in front of the Atlantic Garage and Service Station at Ninth Place and G Street, the site of the Martin Luther King Jr. Memorial Library today. Since gas rationing left the station virtually vacant, Blake told a newspaper reporter in August 1942 that he had time to attend to the garden and "picked about five pounds of string beans from the garden in the first two months alone."

Employees of the National Housing Agency demonstrate how a Victory Garden can be created from a vacant urban lot in Washington. Pictured in April 1943 are, from left to right, Dorothy Boyce, Burtha Naylor, Mrs. and Mr. Milton Newman, and Rosa Keeter. The influx of new residents from rural communities assisted in creation of such gardens in the urban core of Washington. Incidentally, a vacant lot in the 2200 block of S Street, N.W., purchased by the German government in 1923 for a new embassy, was converted to one of the more popular Victory Gardens in the city.

Mrs. Cora Flagg, a member of the Oxon Run Victory Garden Club, works a weeder in the Oxon Run Garden, located near the D.C. line in Southeast, on June 3, 1943. Typical gardens featured rows of tomatoes, cucumbers, corn, beets, and beans.

Stanley Smith of Bethesda does his part in growing a successful Victory Garden outside his Maryland home. His picture appeared in the May 8, 1944, edition of the *Washington Star*. Fearing that a German sympathizer was behind every plate of sauerkraut, the vegetable was referred to as "Liberty Cabbage."

This resident of Southwest Washington overlooks her Victory Garden, while proudly displaying two stars in her window denoting that two men in the family were serving as part of the war effort. As late as December 1944, the government announced that all chickens produced in Virginia, West Virginia, and Delaware would be bought by the Army Quartermaster Corps. (LOC.)

Five

THE WOMAN WORKFORCE

World War II offered the opportunity for women to become full-time income producers en masse, unlike any other period in the history of the United States. Many heeded the government's call to come to Washington, rent a room, and work proudly in one of the hundreds of thousands of new jobs created during the war years. Women were trained to perform many of the jobs that had previously been held exclusively by men, as Rosie the Riveter became a symbol of the capabilities of all wartime female employees.

Women also enlisted in the military through the Women's Auxiliary Army Corps (WAACs), the Lady Marines, and the Women Appointed for Voluntary Service (WAVES). Col. Oveta Hobby would take control of the WAACs in July 1941, and would eventually lead a force of 150,000 women stationed in Washington and throughout the world.

Meanwhile, Washingtonians opened their doors and rented rooms to the ever-increasing numbers of women arriving in the city. Many became fully entrenched in government work, and for many, it was a new opportunity to become self-sufficient. Many, sadly, also became war widows as their husbands were killed in action.

World War II in Washington also provided unheard-of opportunity for African-American women to find employment and housing in what was then a segregated city. The Lucy Stowe Hall had been built just south of Howard University, and offered the latest in designs and accommodations for black women arriving in the city with hopes of finding government jobs. Many enlisted in the WAACs, as Colonel Hobby had mandated that it be open to the proportionate number of black women as was found in the general population, a truly bold move on her part in the era.

Col. Oveta Culp Hobby (right) is seen here in 1943 talking with Auxiliary Margaret Peterson and Captain Gilbert at Mitchel Field, located just outside New York City. Practicing law in Texas, she had been brought to Washington in September 1941 by General Marshall to head the Women's Auxiliary Army Corps (WAACs), which would grow to 10,000 women in its first year. It was expected to reach 150,000 by 1944. She was integral in finding jobs in the military that women could perform, and rigid in her uniform requirements, one of which would affectionately be coined the "Hobby Hat." (World Telegram & Sun Photo by Al Aumuller, LOC.)

Miss Margaret Duffy was one of the first female employees of the U.S. Weather Bureau, hired in 1942. Mr. C.O. Schick, then the meteorologist in charge, stated in the April 23, 1942, *Washington Star* that "he had always been opposed to women as weather workers, but he has been surprised—they will learn every phase of observation, but will not be allowed to make formal forecasts, which is a ticklish feat." Duffy can be seen here launching a weather balloon from Washington National Airport. Not shown is the radiosonde, which is attached to the helium balloon when released, broadcasting temperature, humidity, and pressure readings. When the balloon finally pops, the instrument descends by parachute, with note attached asking for its return. It was noted in the *Star* article "that if the radiosonde should fall on an axis submarine near the coast it would do its captors no good, for it forgets its weather findings as soon as it has broadcast."

A poster of Gen. Douglas MacArthur hangs on the wall of the Army Photographic Library in 1942 to inspire the female government workers in the temporary Main Navy and Munitions Building near the Mall. The WAACs identified 54 jobs that women could perform, freeing up combat-fit soldiers to head to the front lines.

Evalyn Walsh McLean, owner of the Hope Diamond, sent her butler Gustave Grifoni out to the bus stop near her lavish estate on Wisconsin Avenue, N.W., in north Cleveland Park to offer government girls a refreshing drink of water when this photograph was taken on July 26, 1942.

This female test crew was photographed on July 9, 1942, at the Aberdeen Proving Grounds testing a 40-mm automatic antiaircraft gun. Women from every state were employed at the Grounds and ranged from high school girls to grandmothers.

Miss Inez Braddy is only one of dozens of women that studied welding at the National Defense Training School in the old Harbor Garage, located at Ninth and H Streets, S.W. Colonel Hobby of the WAACs broke racial lines when she encouraged African-American women to join the ranks, the first of whom did so in September 1940, following a two-month training session in Fort Des Moines, Iowa.

These women are seen receiving instruction at a Washington, D.C., war production plant. The Marines had an equivalent to the WAAC, coined the Lady Marines. It was headed by Ruth Cheney Streeter, who commanded 18,000 enlisted women and 1,000 female officers by July 1944.

One of the many women working at the Navy Department is seen here at the Navy Yard. The Navy Department had appointed Mildred Helen McAfee as the Women Appointed for Voluntary Emergency Service, or WAVES, in August 1942. She applied harsh rules, including a no-dating rule except when one was on leave, only enough make-up "to look human," and no smoking on the streets. By mid-May 1944, almost half of the uniformed personnel at the Naval Headquarters in Washington were women.

Women were put to work performing a wide variety of duties, and one Navy Department memo stated in May 1944 that 158 WAVES had filled the jobs of 163 men. They worked as photographers, operated control towers, and even learned the bugle, relieving the local male musicians for more hazardous duty overseas. The leader of the WAACs, Col. Oveta Hobby, was the first woman to receive the Distinguished Service Medal.

These women were photographed enthusiastically registering for the WAACs draft for women, which eventually numbered more than 150,000. Colonel Hobby stated that women should replace men in non-combat duty, and if necessary fight, all while being subject to the discipline that their male counterparts endured.

WAC Barracks
BOLLING FIELD, D.C.

These rows of temporary barracks were built for the exclusive use of women enlisted in the WAAC, and were located at Bolling Field, which later became Bolling Air Force Base, in Southeast Washington.

The National Office of Civilian Defense receives its shipment of 13,270 helmets to be distributed to city residents as part of the Metropolitan Civilian Defense program. Seen here are Paul Keen, District Property Officer, and Mrs. Nell Holmes, assistant director of the National Office.

Sister Aquinas, nicknamed the "flying nun," was originally from Ironwood, Michigan, and held a pilot's license with many hours of flying on her record. She spent time during the war training fellow nuns in various aircraft maintenance and flying at Washington National Airport. This field trip of the "flying nun" pre-flight class took place at its hangers in June 1943. Sister Aquinas is seen here explaining the engine structure of an aircraft to her students. (Photo by Ann Rosener, LOC.)

Women also worked as auxiliary police in the city, as many of its male police officers were drafted into duty. This pair was photographed at the police headquarters building at Fourth and Constitution Avenue, N.W.

Mrs. Gladys Pawielski, who had become a war widow after she started driving for the Railway Express, leaps off her truck with a package she collected on her Connecticut Avenue route on November 12, 1943.

Seen here is the Potomac Electric Power Company telephone exchange with the building telephone warden, C.L. Herbert, right, conferring with Mrs. Melton, chief operator. Operators often practiced civil defense drills while on the job.

War workers at the Treasury Department were charged with recording millions of "Series E War Savings Bonds" serial numbers by hand in these cumbersome ledgers. In 1944, its peak year of sales, the Treasury sold bonds to 27 million individuals, representing a total investment of over $12 billion. That also meant recording 27 million serial numbers, with blank space left to the right of each entry to be filled out with the date and location of redemption.

This female wartime worker is seen at the Navy Yard performing a turning operation on a heavy 36-inch engine lathe. Unique captured German, Japanese, and Italian guns were often sent to the Navy Yard for analysis by naval experts stationed at the Yard. (World Wide Photos.)

Women's Auxiliary Army Corps stationed at the Pentagon march past a review stand at Fort Myer, while Col. K.P. Cooley (front), Commanding Officer of the Post; Brig. Gen. Robert N. Young; and Benjamin M. McKelway, associate editor of the *Washington Star*, look on. The image was captured on September 6, 1945.

Mrs. Effie Hansbrough, left, of 214 North Columbus Street in Alexandria, Virginia, and Mrs. Mary Frances Powell check and straighten rocket fins on motor tubes at the Navy Yard. The image ran in the *Washington Star* on June 20, 1948. Following the war, the Navy Yard became a primary research and development installation.

Six

TEMPORARY BUILDINGS AND THE HOUSING SHORTAGE

Washington had been suffering from a shortage of both office space and housing since World War I, when the giant Main Navy and Munitions Building had been built as one of the city's first temporary structures, at Seventeenth and Constitution Avenue, N.W. Following the declaration of war, thousands of Americans were called to Washington to aid in the effort, most finding work in a wooden and drafty office building, built hurriedly on open land on the National Mall, and connected together in a maze of wooden ramps and overpasses.

These buildings were cheap and easy to build and literally sprang up overnight in some cases. By 1943, nearly the entire area of the Mall was covered with these buildings, and the government looked to build additional facilities in the city's traffic circles, and in distant Arlington, Virginia. Even the construction of the world's largest permanent office building, the Pentagon, which opened in 1942, did little to relieve cramped office space, with most stenographers working side by side in an office with a hundred personnel or more; what the collective volume of all those manual typewriters must have sounded like is anyone's guess.

On the home front, Washingtonians opened their large townhouses and began renting out affordable rooms to the woman work force and to military personnel. Grand ballrooms were floored over and transformed into offices, while other large estates, such as the McLeans' Friendship, were torn down altogether to make room for much needed apartment space.

Following the war, many of these temporary buildings were disassembled and used for a time on the country's college campuses, including Georgetown University, which swelled with new students utilizing the G.I. Bill. The 'temporary' Main Navy and Munitions Building actually had a rather long life: it survived nearly 60 years on the National Mall, and wasn't torn down until the early 1970s.

The Main Navy and Munitions Building was built in 1918 on Constitution Avenue, N.W., on the Mall north of the Lincoln Memorial reflecting pool; an additional floor was built during World War II. Built in just six months, it covered 1.8 million square feet, all atop more than 5,000 foundation pilings. It housed 14,000 workers. (Courtesy National Portrait Gallery.)

Even the golf course at the National War College on Fort Leslie J. McNair in Southwest Washington was targeted for temporary housing, and in this case, it was surveyed and found to be suitable for 5,000 housing units in the spring of 1941.

The Navy Department built a series of massive buildings in Arlington, Virginia, seen here on their opening day, August 1, 1941. They were built to house a total of 7,000 office workers at a total cost of $3.2 million. They later were used as an annex to the Pentagon, which began construction later that fall.

The Navy Department was faced with the challenge of building temporary buildings with little or no metal and other materials conserved for the war effort. Wide use of concrete was institutionalized, utilizing sand dredged from the bottom of the Potomac. The interior courtyards of the Navy's large building in Arlington, north of where the Pentagon would be built, are seen here. The long rows of building sections were connected by passageways on several different levels.

The Navy Department built a series of buildings in a similar fashion to what would evolve as the Pentagon, at the intersection of Columbia Pike and Arlington Ridge Road. They were photographed for the *Washington Star* on November 1, 1941, shortly after they opened and only a month before Pearl Harbor.

Built in 1942 on the site of what is today Freedom Plaza, this temporary building housed an amalgamation of informational booths for myriad governmental departments aimed at recently arrived businessmen, servicemen, government workers, and contractors. Its official mission was to "smooth the path for citizens coming to Washington on business with the government under confused and congested wartime conditions."

The Information Center on what is today's Freedom Plaza was the brainchild of Lowell Mellett, who had been accused of being Roosevelt's propagandist. Within the building, confusion generally reigned, so much so that the managing editor of the *Washington Post*, Alexander F. Jones, called it "Mellett's Madhouse" in an editorial. The name stuck, and people thereafter referred to the Information Center as the "Madhouse." The temporary quarters of the Defense Housing Registry can be seen in front of the District Building on Pennsylvania Avenue when this image was taken on February 8, 1942. (Author's private collection.)

George Washington University lent ground near Washington Circle for the erection of this center, built for visiting servicemen on weekends, housing a total of 500 enlisted men. Housing shortages continued even after D-Day, with the Defense Department announcing that in June 1944 alone, 2,600 additional government girls were expected to arrive in Washington.

The temporary buildings on the Mall can be seen to the west of the Washington Monument in this 1943 image; the World War I–era Main Navy and Munitions Building is in the background with a series of 17 500-foot-long wings housing 14,000 workers. Over 30,000 employees worked in temporary buildings constructed on the Mall in World War II, with many of the buildings lasting until 1971. (LOC.)

Seen from atop the Washington Monument, the enormity of the complete set of temporary buildings on the Mall is clearly evident. They performed a variety of duties, from office space for the War Department during the construction of the Pentagon to housing for recently arrived government personnel. While a few of these remained in place until the early 1970s, many were taken down following the war and reconstructed at the nation's universities and small towns.

The ballroom of the Leiter mansion at 1500 New Hampshire Avenue, N.W., on Dupont Circle, was the scene of many important Washington social events. Like most large mansions in and around Washington, it was transformed for war effort work. In this case, the ballroom was configured for the stenographer pool of the National Advisory Committee on Aeronautics when this image was taken on August 25, 1943. The house was later demolished.

The section of the Mall in front of the newly opened National Gallery of Art was slated to be used for the housing for 1,200 government workers when this image was taken on May 7, 1941.

A prefabricated house, proposed for housing government workers, was put on display on the Mall in May 1941. It could be built in just six days and was composed of only a few strips of metal, with canvas interior partitions.

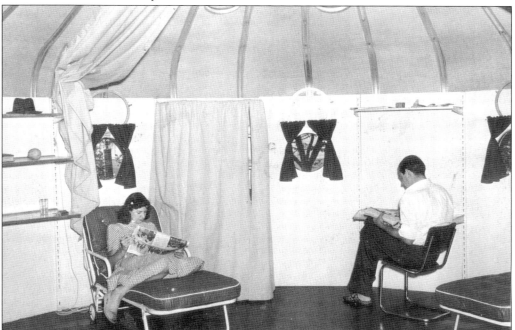

The interior of the proposed metal housing project was partitioned with canvas. The entire structure could be built for just $750. It is unknown how many were actually built; this was just one of many examples presented by hopeful contractors wishing for a massive government contract to provide cheap housing.

These government girls, who had been working at the Home Owners Loan Corporation, were photographed on September 18, 1941, the day they prepared to transfer to a military job in New York City. The Washington metro area was already facing a housing shortage before the war, as its population had risen from approximately 200,000 two decades prior to the attack on Pearl Harbor to nearly 700,000 at the beginning of 1941.

Many area residents answered the call by the government to provide rooms in their townhouses for arriving government girls and servicemen. It also offered a source of income for the city's residents and was seen as the patriotic thing to do during the war years. Thousands of advertisements began to appear in the City Directories and newspapers offering rooms in homes along almost every block of the city.

A staunch supporter of the war effort, Evalyn Walsh McLean sold her estate, Friendship, on December 31, 1941, to the government for $1 million and moved to a house at 3308 R Street, N.W., in Georgetown. The lavish mansion served as construction crew headquarters when this photograph was taken in 1942, showing the massive housing being constructed on its former gardens. The site is known today as McLean Gardens along a long stretch of Wisconsin Avenue, N.W., at the edge of Cleveland Park.

The first Washington-area home purchased by the National Housing Agency for conversion into apartments for war workers was this rundown townhouse at 908–910 Cameron Street in Alexandria, Virginia. It was purchased from Brig. Gen. Duncan Major in November 1942 and remodeled at a cost of $5,000. It was one of 260 applications received by that date for possible conversions, with the Agency providing grants for conversion.

A series of raids in Washington's known houses of prostitution was held in November 1942. The military personnel seen here were turned over to their service authorities. In March 1943, residents were shocked to learn that two five-room apartments configured as an office known as the "Institute" at the Wardman Park Hotel in Woodley Park was actually a large brothel, operating for years in their midst. The FBI seized a "rating book" naming its distinguished clientele and listing their prowess and preferences, which has never been released.

This building at Third and U Street, N.W., opened at a cost of $760,000 on December 15, 1942, and was called the Lucy D. Slowe Hall, named after an educator and the first black women's tennis champion in the United States. It was constructed for the exclusive purpose of housing African-American female government workers. By January 12, 1943, the building was only 50 percent occupied, despite the severe shortage of housing for workers in Washington, which created an outcry among area leaders.

The main lobby of the Lucy Slowe Hall in LeDroit Park is seen here with its occupants in 1943. The building contained 277 single rooms, which rented for $7 per week, and 22 double rooms, priced at $6 per person per week. Its was managed by W. Spurgeon Burke on behalf of the Defense Homes Corporation, and targeted African-American women that had been in Washington less than a year. The agency expected an additional 35,000 such women to descend on the city between January and July 1943.

Any vacant public park or land was subject to being taken over for defense housing, as was this location along Route 1 near Alexandria, Virginia, which housed mobile trailers set up for defense workers. Office buildings were sometimes taken over as well, such as the well-known Apex Building at Constitution Avenue and Seventh Street, N.W., which served as the Office of Naval Intelligence beginning in 1942.

Housing that could be built in only five weeks seemed to spring up everywhere in and around Washington, including these temporary housing structures built on the Arlington Experimental Farm grounds in Virginia. They were torn down in the 1960s, and the land was annexed by Arlington National Cemetery for use as mass gravesites. (NA.)

Many D.C. residents solved the problem of finding suitable housing during World War II by purchasing or renting houseboats. Temporarily anchored due to gas rationing, hundreds of such boats lined the city's harbors. Seen here in the summer of 1943 is the director of the Government Girls School for Self Improvement, Mrs. John Paul Gensener, and her son John.

The Capitol Park Hotel at Union Station Plaza was taken over by the Federal Works Agency and converted to a servicemen's residential center and officers' lounge. One of many such hotel conversions to be found citywide, as noted by the sign, all guests had to vacate by August 31, 1943.

John N. Blanford, National Housing Administrator, looks over one of the models of a Victory House being shown at the Small Homes Embassy at 2129 S Street, N.W. The potential home's design was displayed in answer to the government's plea for defense housing; this particular model priced at about $6,000.

This image of the National Mall was taken on June 6, 1949, showing the extent of the Mall that had been taken over for the construction of temporary buildings. City officials had hoped to remove many of the buildings by the time of the Sesquicentennial of Washington in 1950, but many would remain for decades. Seen at left is the Main Navy Building, which was still home to 10,500 national defense employees as late as 1953. To the right of the reflecting pool were a series of buildings that housed occupants "too secret to mention" according to the *Washington Star* that year.

The temporary buildings on the Mall at Seventeenth and Constitution, N.W., were not torn down until September 1964, when they were photographed by Bob Burchette of the *Washington Post*.

The demolition of the massive Navy Munitions Building was captured on August 18, 1970. It had functioned as a "tempo" since its beginnings in World War I.

Seven

VE, VJ Day, and the War's Aftermath

With the announcement of the unconditional German surrender in May 1945, Washingtonians took to the streets to celebrate, as did the rest of the country. However, it was noted that the city residents celebrated in a more muted tone than New York City residents, perhaps knowing that many of their loved ones would return from Europe only to be sent off to fight in the Pacific theater. With VJ Day declared in August 1945, however, the city's streets once again became crowed with jubilant residents who celebrated until dawn.

Washington following World War II was forever changed, with new suburban housing communities being constructed and the headquarters of all the military services entrenched in the Pentagon. Returning GIs faced a severe work and housing shortage, many of whom came home with "War Brides" they had met in Europe. One such individual was Nada Diana Coates, who married American Corporal William V. Harless at Neubiberg Air Force Base, located outside Munich, in 1946. Like many Europeans, she immigrated to the United States, taught herself the language, worked in the medical field, and eventually became a naturalized citizen. Her accounts of life during and after the war in Europe are spellbinding.

Another group headed to Washington after the war were the captured German scientists, brought under a program coined the Operation Paperclip. The author's mother worked for such an individual under secrecy at the Naval Weapons Center, an underwater explosion expert named Dr. Hans Snay.

Washington also set out to memorialize the thousands who lost their lives in the war, with many buried at Arlington National Cemetery. The official World War II Memorial was dedicated on the Mall at a ceremony on Memorial Day 2004, a long overdue tribute to the men and women who protected the United States and liberated most of Europe.

With war in Europe over, the city residents turned their attention to another pending doom—the evolution into the Cold War period. Washington's ground zero milestone on the ellipse, just south of the White House, went from a milestone measuring road distances to and from Washington to its symbol as a nuclear target.

This group portrait of the Dumbarton Oaks conference was taken in August 1944. Representatives from the United States, Great Britain, Russia, and China met for seven weeks beginning in the summer of 1944 at the Georgetown estate to plan for peace and the recovery of Europe following the war. At the end of the secret meeting, they resolved that an organization known as the United Nations be created that could take "such action by air, naval, or land forces as may be necessary to maintain or restore international peace." A preliminary charter was drawn up to be disseminated at future meetings in San Francisco. (LOC.)

Fresh into his fourth term, and just a month before VE Day, President Roosevelt died suddenly on the afternoon of April 12, 1945, and Vice President Harry Truman became the nation's 33rd President. Roosevelt's funeral procession is seen here on April 14, 1945, along Delaware Avenue, en route to the White House. (World Wide Photos, MLK Library.)

Through a famous Associated Press scoop, the world learned that Germany had surrendered unconditionally in the early hours of May 7, 1945; the official announcement was made by the joint Allies at 9 a.m., on May 8th, Victory in Europe Day. A soldier and his daughter read about the surrender of Germany in the *Evening Star* while sitting in front of the White House. The *Washington Post* had noted that the city's residents were rather subdued in their reaction compared to New Yorkers, suggesting that they knew from more first-hand experience that a formidable foe was still waging war in the Pacific.

The German Embassy on Massachusetts Avenue, N.W., near Thomas Circle, had been transferred to the neutral Swiss government for the duration of the war. With the unconditional surrender of the Axis powers and the loss of diplomatic identity, the State Department confiscated the embassy and its contents. Officials are seen here in May 1945 substituting a State Department sign for that of the former embassy. (NA.)

The U.S. government took over the German Embassy following its long vacancy during the war, when the building was maintained by the Swiss government. Only furniture and paintings remained when this image was taken on May 23, 1945.

Soldiers, WAACs, nurses, medical corpsmen, and civilian employees at Walter Reed Army Hospital were jubilant in their first reaction to the news of the German surrender on May 8, 1945. President Truman described it as a "solemn but glorious hour" in his announcement to the American people that day.

Gen. Dwight D. Eisenhower is seen here acknowledging the cheers of onlookers during his triumphal parade through Washington, held on June 18, 1945. His procession stopped before the north entrance of the District Building, where he was presented with a key to the city. He replied with the statement that "all my years as commander-in-chief, all my life, I have never been so proud and so thankful as to have been given the key to the capital city of my country."

In preparation for the possible announcement that war with Japan was officially over, barriers were placed in front of the White House as they had been on VE Day. This image from the August 10, 1945, *Washington Star* shows military police redirecting pedestrian traffic away from Pennsylvania Avenue, with the State Department in the background.

President Harry Truman will always be known as the commander-in-chief who made the decision to drop the atomic bomb on Hiroshima on August 6, 1945, and a second "big boy" on the city of Nagasaki on August 9th, leveling the entire metropolitan areas and killing their residents. The Japanese government surrendered, and Truman held a press conference on August 14, 1945, announcing the surrender and declaring it Victory in Japan Day.

Upon hearing the news from President Truman that Japan had surrendered, a conga line formed in Lafayette Park, opposite the White House, calling for the President to join in. Washingtonians were finally allowed to celebrate the end of World War II. (LOC.)

This image was taken in Washington on August 14, 1945, with residents and soldiers celebrating VJ Day.

This image was taken by a *Washington Star* photographer on August 14, 1945, looking west on F Street, N.W., showing revelers celebrating VJ Day.

Jubilant Washingtonians celebrate the Japanese surrender on August 14, 1945, announced at 7 p.m. that day by President Truman.

VJ Day is celebrated on the streets of Washington.

Victorious crowds are seen here on the city streets celebrating VJ Day in 1945. (LOC.)

These revelers were photographed on Washington's streets by the *Washington Star* celebrating VJ Day.

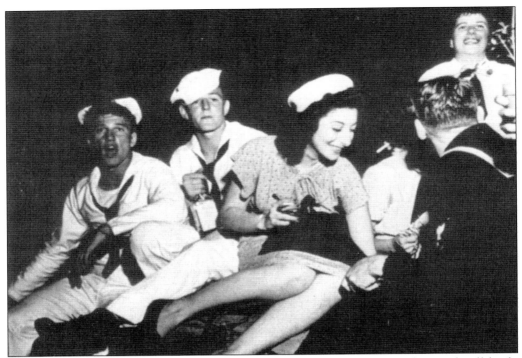

The announcement of VJ Day was also obviously a cause for celebrating with a good stiff drink, as these obviously intoxicated sailors and a female war worker were photographed on the city street riding on the hood of a car. (NA.)

On the day of the announcement of the Japanese surrender, August 14, 1945, crowds swelled in front of the White House to await an address of President Truman, given from the front porch when the house was under renovation. (World Wide Photos, MLK Library.)

An estimated crowd of 7,500 gathered at the Capitol Building on September 23, 1945, to cheer General Wainwright the day he addressed both the House and the Senate.

These warships docked at the Washington Navy Yard in October 1945, shortly after the Japanese surrender. Today, much of the local naval troop movement takes place in Norfolk, Virginia instead of the Navy Yard, due to its proximity to the Capitol and the excessive silt that has obscured large shipping routes in the northern Potomac. (LOC.)

Marines in full battle regalia face the Capitol as they prepare to take their place in the Admiral Chester W. Nimitz Parade on October 6, 1945.

This Nimitz Day parade view was taken from atop the Treasury Building as units moved up Pennsylvania Avenue.

Thousands of Washingtonians gathered on the Washington Monument grounds to review the parade and hear comments from Admiral Nimitz. The speaker's platform (upper center) was set against a backdrop depicting the battleship *Missouri*.

Construction of the National Archives building began in 1933, the first time the government institutionalized a central repository for its vast documents. Truck convoys continued for months following the war, seen here dropping off a voluminous amount of paperwork that stemmed from the war effort and from many of the temporary buildings that were demolished beginning in 1945.

Seen here is the vast library of the National War College, built in 1903 as the Army War College, located on the southern tip of Fort Lesley J. McNair in Southwest Washington. Established near the confluence of the Anacostia and Potomac Rivers, it was originally designed to protect Washington from river invasions and is the oldest Army post in the country in existence today. On February 21, 1903, President Theodore Roosevelt laid the cornerstone to the main building that now bears his name. It has been home to the Army War College (1903–1917, 1919–1940), War Plans Division, War Department General Staff, Selective Service System Headquarters, and Headquarters for the U.S. Army Ground Forces (all successively during World War II), before being coined the National War College in 1946. It continues to serve in that capacity today. (LOC.)

During Veterans Housing Week in May 1946, this float demonstrated the need for housing veterans that remained without homes, encouraging anyone with a room or apartment for rent to contact the government Housing Center, then located at 1400 Pennsylvania Avenue, N.W.

The new veterans' housing project at Portland and South Capitol Streets, S.E., was dedicated on September 6, 1946. The 80-unit project was one of many planned to provide much-needed housing for returning veterans that had been created from renovated and relocated former temporary buildings originally constructed for the Army.

The post-war housing need for returning GIs resulted in the ingenuity on several fronts; seen here is a predecessor of the large mobile home, a housing unit that could be transported while its bedroom units were telescoped inward and easily unloaded by the use of a boom. It was named a Wingfoot Home, manufactured by a company of the same name.

A group of potential purchasers are shown entering the War Assets Administration Customer Service Center building on its opening day, March 10, 1947. Thousands of surplus war items were sold and auctioned in the years following the war.

A group of New York college girls who called themselves "The Widows to Be of World War Three" picketed in front of the White House on May 13, 1947, seeking a Congressional investigation of American industrialists that had been involved with their German counterparts that were about to go on trial in Germany for war crimes. Pictured here are, from left to right. Betty Horowitz, Judy Manner, Gloria Toren, Elaine Dulgov, and Barbara Dechter.

The public was invited to experience a simulated ship's deck set up during an open house at the Naval Yard that took place on October 27, 1947.

The famed Iwo Jima memorial in Arlington was photographed during its installation in 1954. Its design was created by sculptor Felix de Weldon, fashioned from a photograph taken by Associated Press photographer Joe Rosenthal. The event memorialized was that of the ultimate victory against Japanese Imperial forces, who had been entrenched on the island of Iwo Jima, at a cost of over 24,000 American marines over a period of 36 days in 1945. (NA.)

With the end of World War II, Washington and the country entered a new era of war, the Cold War, which was to last nearly four decades. Three workers with the District Chapter of the Red Cross are seen here beginning to dig a fire trench in a disaster mass-feeding drill held on July 13, 1956, at Third and K Street, S.W. The drill was held in anticipation of possible Cold War-era invasion or emergency. Seen are, from left to right, Mrs. George Calver, Mrs. Elizabeth Bass, and Mrs. Carl Erickson.

Many of those who lost their lives fighting for America were buried overseas, near the spot where they lost their lives. Thousands more, however, were interred in the Arlington National Cemetery in Arlington, Virginia, seen here. On Memorial Day 2004, a World War II Memorial was dedicated, at long last, on the National Mall just west of the Washington Monument.